I Have No Idea

What I'm Doing

Candy Aragon

DEDICATION

I dedicate this book and everything else I will ever publish to my

familia whom I love more than anything in the world.

WHATS INSIDE?

ACKNOWLEDGMENTS

Moroni, thank you for **always** having my back despite all my imperfections. Your unconditional love and admiration has been my motivation to become a better me and find ways to better the world. I love you and I like you. =)

Mami y Papi, LOS AMO. Thank you for believing in me and for your support throughout all the stages of my life. I am super blessed to have you as my parents and for the life you have given my sisters and I.

To my sisters, thank you for being born and making me a big sister ;) You guys are my inspiration and I love you guys so much you don't even know!!

And shout out to my dog Link, who can't read but helps me keep my sanity every day.

Without any of you, this book would not have been possible.

I Love you all!! Gracias!!

Preface

We live in an era that's impossible to follow and everything seems to just fall on peoples laps; stress, responsibilities, self-doubt, family issues, and debt! We don't seem to be getting anywhere near where we would like our lives to be. However, we still see many people becoming successful and living their best life. So what do all these successful people do to live their lives how they want to? How are they surviving in these complicated times? Who do they talk to? What about you? Do your dreams seem so ridiculously out of reach now that you just settle? Are you drowning in unwanted problems? Have you lowered your standards to live a comfortable life? What's something that's consuming your time and money that you wish you could delete like a Facebook friend?

This book is written by someone who is asking herself all those questions. Just a random wife in her late 20s sitting at home, with a laptop and lots to say. So I'm probably not the most qualified person to tell you how to live your life OR maybe I'm the only person who can….. Who knows? But if you keep reading and maybe waste your time here instead of your Facebook feed, I promise you it'll be 10000% more effective (in some way) than putting it down to get back to your streaming shows. Just saying.

If you choose the path of impulsive curiosity and check out this book I promise to make your life a little better, if I don't then you can never buy a book from me again. If you choose the path of skepticism then maybe this book is exactly for you! Either way I win. So just do it.

In the following pages I will go over what principles or habits (whatever you want to call them) I have learned that led me to get my act together, think out of the box and write this book. So here we go!

(Warning, all literature and English profession people, I apologize in advance for my lack of proper punctuation, grammar and any other mistake I may have made, just keepin' it real.)

Chapter 1

Turn it off

Since I was a little innocent child my daily routine was usually the same. It changed a bit as I grew older and got married. Growing up it was School, Homework, TV and Sleep, I'd eat somewhere in between. Then as an unbearable adolescent it was School, homework, chat, TV, sleep. Once I started college, It was school, homework, and sleep. Cause the universe knows there was no way in heck our professors would let us have enough time to do anything else, including nourishing our bodies. Now as a married adult in my late 20s and having moved to a different state and no job, my routine is; wakeup, Zumba, clean, shower, write, cook, TV or video games and sleep. Sounds like a pretty sweet schedule for a woman in her late 20's right? I'm not going to lie, it is pretty sweet.

However, before I started being able to have this kind of life I was a business owner for a bakery and having to deal with my own employees and work place drama, then I was a substitute teacher having to deal with someone else's students and adolescent drama AND if I wasn't at work I would still have to hear about family drama. So being in another state and not having to work for a while has been like heaven to me. Thankfully I married someone who was easily tricked into doing most of the work, so its not a huge deal that I'm not currently working...lets hope he never reads this. Anyway, Where was I going with this? Oh Right, Once we moved and I got zero responses from the 20 plus jobs I applied to, I had enough time to start thinking "what the heck am I doing with my life?!" I felt stuck in this routine and had no idea what to do. No jobs I wanted, no career path I was super passionate about.

All my friends and family members who were my age seemed to have their career plan and knew what they wanted to accomplish. There was also the problem that most "entry level" jobs require a person in their 20s to have ten plus years of experience working in a position that requires you to have a degree that took you five plus years to get. So the math doesn't really add up, unless you've held that degree since before you graduated high school... so, what the heck was I supposed to do? I started to feel defeated and frustrated.

That's when I decided I needed to turn everything off and think for a moment. I turned off my TV, I turned off my laptop, my phone, the pressure from others, I turned off my negative thinking, my self-doubt and the lack of motivation I had. It all went off. I asked myself "What is something I wish I could do?" Not something I want to do or should or have, but wish.

When we think of the word wish its usually referring to something that's almost impossible. For example, "I wish I could live in Disneyland and eat all the chimichangas I want." (Its kind of my impossible wish), that's usually what a wish sounds like. So I changed the word from wish to dream. What was my dream? My dream is to become the best version of myself, to be a very well known person in our time, make lots of money, help others and to better the culture of my generation. By well known I don't necessarily mean famous or 'Intsafamous'. I just wanted to create a platform for myself. I realized I have so much to offer and wanted to do something about it. Sounds like a long shot, doesn't it?

Then I asked myself the second question; "What do I need to do to get there?" , this one was hard. I knew I was not 'attractive enough' or talented enough to be a model or actress or singer. I didn't study anything that could get me into the mainstream media AND I was not charming and funny enough to become a comedian or social media famous. I didn't know how to be a better me, and I sure as heck didn't know what aspect of our culture I wanted to change.

So I began to write down things I was good at and people who can possibly help me. On that list of things I noticed I was good at ranting and voicing my thoughts and opinions on things I was passionate about. I also noticed I loved writing even though I was not very good at it, I loved it. It was like having a conversation with myself. So I began writing a book. Not this book, a children's book. It did not take me very long to write it and once I did it made me feel like I could take on the world. Of course that feeling disappeared instantly when I realized I needed to find an illustrator, edit it and publish it if I wanted to get something out of it. The little pessimistic demon angel thing came out and reassured me that it was going to be difficult AND expensive. I let it talk me down for a little but then I turned that little chizz off. I went ahead and Googled "how to publish a children's book." Once I got that down I moved on to the next thing; Writing another one.

As far as this book goes and we're keeping it as real as possible, I though of it while I was sitting on the toilet and thought to myself "there is so much I have learned in the past 6 months and Its changed my life completely I need to share it with the world." So if this a learning book then I guess you could say this is lesson #1 to your better self: TURN IT OFF. Whatever it may be. Negative thoughts, negative people telling you your dream is stupid and only a few lucky ones get to live it.

TURN OFF your Facebook app, or whatever other social site you see and read bad news on, its just makes you angry and distracts you from being rational and possibly giving you the opportunity to do something about it. TURN OFF your tv set for a while. Don't get me wrong I don't trust people who claim they don't watch TV but I do believe that all things must be in small doses. Too much cake gives you diabetes, well too much TV or social media makes you idle to your full potential.

When we live life to the fullest, its not about going skydiving (which I've done and you should definitely try it) but about living to your fullest ability. If you're good at drawing but work as a customer service rep turn off that little voice telling you you're stuck there because you need the money, or because you're too old to do art and go sign up for an evening art or animation class. You can still become a famous painter or work for an animation studio. If you want to give a shot at acting, go audition. If you cant act then maybe consider getting a job working around actors at a studio of some kind. If you always wanted to teach but haven't been able to go to college, take a part time job as teacher assistant and take some evening classes. If you've always wanted to travel, start by getting your passport and talk to your boss about how many vacation days you get a year and accumulate them. You're not dead, so you can still work for and live out your dreams.

Before I go any further and we are keeping it real, use your common sense when considering your dreams. Yes, your dreams are not impossible and you can always achieve them to a certain extent depending on where you are in life. Don't leave your family or your high paying job that's providing for them just because you want to pursue a dream. Your dreams should also include those whom you love and make sure it doesn't affect them or your relationship with them. If you're single and can do whatever you want then you have an opportunity others may not have and you should go for it, sky is the limit.

Part of this book is keeping track of what you're gaining from it and applying it to your life. For example in this chapter you may have learned that you have some negative things that are taking precious time away from you. So make a list either in a journal or a piece of paper and write down what are some things you can "turn off" for a minute or forever! It could be anything, your TV, your phone, negative people, your own pessimistic thoughts, whatever it may be. Hope you're not bored already, I promise it gets better so don't put me down. STAY!

Chapter 2

Dream/ Your Calling

In the last chapter I mentioned that I had a dream. What do you think of when people ask you "what is your dream?". It could range anywhere from cleaning out your fridge to going on a date with your SO to being a famous opera singer. I have learned that we have been conditioned to shrink our dreams or to settle. For example; when we are little we think about what we want to be or do when we grow up. If you'd ask me when I was 10 what I want to be when I grow up I would have told you "a doctor". Is that unreasonable? No. What did I want to do when I grew up? Well I wanted to help people and make lots of money doing so, so doctor was the most popular and logical option. Lets fast-forward 18 years later. Did I become a doctor? Nope. Am I helping people and making lots of money? I wish! So does that mean I failed? Absolutely it does NOT. But why didn't I become a doctor? For many of us our passions change over time, due to many different factors and circumstances.

I started college with a major in pre-med. I took all my general ed classes the first two semesters. During my second semester I had to take a college chemistry class. I really thought I was going to do well, given the fact that I had straight A's in high school and did very well in my chemistry class. Well, no one tells you that your brain decides to throw things out when you don't use them anymore, or deletes any useless information whenever it wants. Long story short, I got a D in that class. That D defined the rest of my college life. To make things worse the next semester I got an F in my college algebra class and I thought I was going to die. Because if my parents ever found out I had an F in college that would have been the end of me. Luckily I was an adult who made her own class schedule and I don't think they knew until probably right now as they read this. Once I realized that my pre-med degree required me to take more science and math classes, I felt defeated. I did not want to spend my life re-taking courses.

So my second year I started it off taking random courses, one of them being psychology. I had never taken a psychology class and didn't really know much about it. After my first class I was hooked. I had found a way I could help people and possibly make lots of money. Since those were the two things I really wanted career-wise I changed my major to social and behavioral sciences and graduated with a B.A. in psychology from California State University, Northridge. There was one problem though, my last semester before graduating I felt like I should have majored in something else. I didn't want to be a therapist or psychologist anymore. I wanted to teach. I later found out that in order to teach you didn't have to have a specific major you just needed to go back to school and get a credential, so that didn't sound too bad.

Not long after I graduated I got a job as a teacher assistant and I loved it. I loved my co-workers, the students and the environment. It has been (so far) the best job I ever had. Unfortunately all good things must come to an end. At the same time my husband and I were operating our own donut franchise so I kind of had two jobs and the second one I absolutely disliked. After working at the school for two years I was faced with a decision, well, it wasn't really a decision, it was inevitable. We had found out that the shopping center where our shop was located was closing and my husband, being the type of person to not waste any time, applied to a great job opportunity that came up.

He was eventually hired and I had no choice but to quit my job at the school to dedicate myself full time to the shop until it closed. Due to some unfortunate events we had to close down earlier than expected. I was sad and a little relieved at the same time. That job brought a lot of stress and anxiety into our lives but it also gave us the ability to buy our house and a new car. Still for the most part it was a good thing that we left early.

After I was free from the shop and unemployed I decided to go back to trying out the teaching thing. At this point we had moved back to my hometown in Lancaster, CA and I applied to be a substitute teacher. What better way to give teaching a trial run, right? I was super excited when I started working, but my excitement did not last very long. I did not think of the fact that being a sub is a little more stressful than being the actual teacher and way more stressful than being a TA. If you're a sub kids will ether love you or hate you. I think this is true for regular teachers as well, but they have time to learn to love the students and vise versa. Subs however only have 6 hours to try and not flip desk on these kids. Some of them were unbearable and others were the best class you could ever meet. The latter was rather rare.

I subbed for about a year and towards the end I took less and less jobs, fearing my day would be too stressful to handle. Then one day my husband gets another **better** job opportunity and we move to Utah. I felt like this was yet again another opportunity for me to change careers. Since I've been in Utah, I've had a chance to re-evaluate my life. Did I really want to teach? Do I want to go back to school and further my psychology education? Or do I want to do something completely risky and live out my dream of helping others and making lots of money?   I had the opportunity to start something new. I had always wanted to find a way to create a platform for myself to effect change in the world. but how? I've established that I was not good at acting or singing. I am not a great painter or sculpture. I don't have the talent to appear as a news anchor or reporter. So then what the heck do I do?? I decided I used my biggest talent and that was sharing my life and ranting.

Writing a book and letting people know they are not the only ones in their late 20's early 30's, 40s etc.. Trying to figure life out. I know there's this social timeline that exist in which we are expected to be at certain points in our life by a certain time. I know people who are younger than me and seem to have their life together and I sometimes wish I had that. Then I realize, maybe it's a good thing I still don't. That just means that all the things I've done until now are just the beginning and not as great as all the things I still have left to do. My life will only get better. Even if you are at a stable job or going to school and on track to graduate but still have another dream in mind, start finding ways to live it out. No matter how unimaginable it may be. If you're a math major and you wish and dream you could be a musician but don't know how to play any instruments, well take a music class and you'll be one step ahead. If you want to be a makeup artist instead of a lawyer, then take a make up class. Start a social media page and put yourself out there. It may not make you as much money as a lawyer AT FIRST. But the student loans will definitely be lower and in the long run you'll be better off because you'll be doing what you **love** not what you **had** to do.

Now, dreams shouldn't just be about what career you want to have, they should also be about what kind of person you aspire to be or what kind of relationships you want to have. Those two are always far more important than how much money you make or your recognition. You can have all the fortune and fame in the world, but when you're alone, with no one to share it with, no one to root for you, its all in vain and you will start dreaming about finding companionship regardless of whether or not you have fame and fortune. They (your companion/family) can be the stepping-stones to something greater than you could have possibly imagined.

Before I was able to start working on my 'career' dream, I needed to work on my personal relationships and my self-love dreams. The top two things that motivated me to really work on my dream are my husband and our parents. I love my husband more than anything and I want our relationship to strengthen and grow. When we were newly-weds we had a lot of issues and arguments over our own selfish and arrogant ways of thinking. We were in our early 20's, of course we were selfish and arrogant. After two years of having pointless fights and living in a stressful environment we evaluated ourselves and realized we needed to focus on learning to love each other.... and ourselves. We worked on ourselves first and used what we learned to understand each other and recognize that we are not the same people and we never will be. We can however love, respect and support each other. Learn something from one another, and recognize that we are a team. Spending a lifetime changing someone else is a waste, because the only person you can really change is yourself. We've learned that over the years, and as you reboot yourself, those around you tend to do that same.

Our parents come into play because one dream my husband and I share is the ability to provide for our families. We both want to accomplish things not so we can buy a huge house or a nice car for ourselves, but to buy our parents the homes and luxuries they have earned. I want to see our parents not have to worry about waking up at 4 in the morning to go to work. They've worked hard to raise us, provide for us, and give us what we needed and sometimes what we wanted, so now it's our turn to return the favor.

Now I am working on living out my dream of starting a small platform. I started a blog to share some of my life stories. I started writing this book with the hopes that many others will read it and gain something from it to help them. I started teaching myself to be open to new things and learned that we can never stop learning, we can never stop dreaming. Once we achieve a goal there's always another and another. Life is limitless. No matter what part of the world you are from, you can live your life how you've always wanted.

So how do you start dreaming? Get your paper and writing utensil and make a list of the things you love and things you don't love. You can categorize it, make a general one about things you love and don't love about your life in general, and one about your job, your lifestyle, your home, your relationship, yourself. You can do a, oh…I don't now.. DREAM BOARD! Actually this can be a rough draft of your dream board.

Starting with baby steps, what are something's you can do this week to better any of those things? For example, maybe you don't like that you and your significant other don't have date nights anymore. Make it a goal to have a date night at least once a week or every two weeks or once a month. It all depends on your resources and time. There is always time to spare. Instead of watching Netflix, go take a walk or have dinner somewhere where you can talk. It'll be hard at first but if one of you keeps being persistent and patient it will become easy. Another example may be that you hate that your job has you clocking in at 4am, now here you have two options, you either find another job or go to bed earlier and train your mind and body to wake up at 4am as if it were 8am. All it is, is change of perspective. If you start off your day with a positive attitude then trust me the rest of your day will turn out completely different than if you drag yourself around all day. Your whole day will be a drag! Not the Sasha Velour kind.

As far as changing something about yourself, its difficult to get rid of old habits, but if you start with maybe cutting down on the cigarettes by one a day or going to the gym once a week and each week go an extra day until you're at five days a week then it wont be as painful. You need to be persistent with yourself like you would with making sure your Wi-Fi is working, make sure your daily goals are working too. these are all small goals, small dreams, I promise that when you focus on these things first you will find the motivation, time and whatever else you need to know exactly what your dream life looks like and work for it. Remember that a dream doesn't have to be career related, it can be related to your profession, family or romantic relationship, your personality, your children, your home, whatever you want!

Its a little cliché and maybe cheesy for some of you to do some of these goal ideas or make a dream board, but if not being cliché and cheesy isn't working out for you then I suggest you put your little prideful self away and try it. It's not going to kill you.

P.S.- If you can't think of a dream or an ambition, use your paper to write down talents you have, or skills. What are you good at? A lot of times we don't all necessarily get to live out a dream, but we live out a calling. Whether or not you know what you want in life we all have a calling to do something. We cant ignore it and we need to use our abilities to fulfill that calling. Maybe its to work or volunteer at a shelter or an orphanage. To work as an educator or maybe you're really good at math and science and whether you desire it or not your calling is to be a medical professional. Its ok not to live out a dream, but its not ok to throw out a calling. There are many people who are living a glamorous life of fame and fortune and still they feel the need to go to college and get an education that may take time away from working towards their fame. Their calling wasn't to become famous, that was just an opportunity towards a dream. They were called to become educated individuals to know how to properly influence their fans and people who admire them. Sooner or later working towards your calling will get you to live a dream life you never even knew you wanted.

Chapter 3

One a day

So, have you picked your goal/dream yet? if you're having a hard time starting your dream board start with something small. For example if one of your dreams is to have a cleaner house then you'd start by doing a house chore. Wash an extra load or wash your dishes right after dinner instead of right before bed. Clear out your dishwasher as soon as its done. If your goal is to have a better relationship with your significant other than maybe you can start with a sweet text like "Hope you're having a great day at work, love you." Or to spice it up "I can't wait to see you tonight." I'm sure they'll like either.

If your goal is bigger picture stuff like quitting your job to find a better one then I suggest applying for another job and setting up interviews, or going to that audition you've been thinking about BEFORE you leave your job. Maybe hire an agent or get your headshots taken if you want to go into the main media. All of those are completely doable. Scary, but doable. One thing I started doing recently was go to the gym regularly. My husband is someone who likes to stay fit and enjoys going to the gym for a little over an hour as much as he can and does his weight exercises. I on the other hand don't really enjoy doing weight training or rep exercise and I definitely don't like spending too much time at gym. I do however love to dance. Back in Lancaster most Zumba classes or any gym with a Zumba class was too pricy so I hardly ever did any kind of physical activity to stay fit.

Luckily we moved to a state where it's definitely more affordable to do things and after my second week here I decided to join a gym specifically to attend its Zumba classes. I started going the last three days of the week. After two weeks I started going five days out of the week, simply because I said I would do it and made a commitment to myself. Just like with writing this book or my blog, I have days where I don't feel like doing absolutely anything and feel like I'm just wasting my time. Then I remember how good it feels to do something productive that you want and feeling accomplished. Trust me, like Nike says; JUST DO IT.

Now if your goal has more to do with changing something about your personality, there are also things you can do little by little. If you want to be more social maybe you can start by smiling at everyone who walks by you, or the person in the car next to you. Then the next day (or week, whenever you're ready) you can wave. Now you're smiling AND waving. Once that becomes a no brainer you're ready to say "hi" or if you're feeling brave enough give them a "good morning, how are you?" I know that may sound scary for someone who just wants to go get their latte and disappear to work and go home without a trace. Trust me, it'll be fun and totally worth it to make eye contact and speak! You got this! For those of you with the opposite problem, maybe you're too outgoing and taking everyone's spotlight, and everyone is starting to find you annoying, there is a cure for that too.

If you find people are giving a sigh every time you're about to tell a story, it usually means that maybe you've said a little more than what people want you to. When in a group convo, try to finish your story and give it maybe like a good 10 seconds for someone else to comment on what you just said or to start a whole different story. Make sure you also listen to what others have to say, don't assume your story is as good as it's going to get. I've noticed that's the case with the super mega talkative socials. They tend to draw their focus towards themselves and ignore what their friends have to say. So maybe just shut up for a minute and give that quiet friend a chance to gather up the courage to say something. Not only will your friendships and other relationships get better but you'll most likely hear some really awesome story you'd wish you'd shut up sooner.

To change your life style you have to be patient, wiling and determined. If you try any of these things and expect results within the first day or even week, you'll be disappointed. You also have to be very consistent and diligent. If you do something different and people are just warming up to it or you're just getting into the grind of things and all of a sudden you stop, trust me there will be disappointments and it will get harder to start up again.

Still, regardless whether you stop or not, the point is to do it again. When you fall or burn yourself on the stove you don't stay on the ground or leave your hand on the hot pan, you get out of the situation and fix the problem. Just like when our Internet all of a sudden stops working, we don't sit around and wait or say "oh well, I didn't need to watch my new episode of this Netflix original anyway." Heck no! We call our Internet provider and make sure the problem gets fixed right then and there. So why cant we be like that with our other more important problems? Go ahead; make yourself the promise that you'll change for the better, give yourself an upgrade.

If you think you've reached the highest level of awesome then you're probably a narcissist and need to change that way of thinking before even your momma cant stand you. We will always have room to grow, change and better ourselves. Don't put your focus on changing the situation. In all honestly, any situation starts with changing yourself first. Like the words of the super mega awesome human being Mr. Michael Jackson, "I'm starting with the man [or women] in the mirror."

Let's Recap

If you haven't gotten one by now, I suggest you get a journal or notebook to write down everything I've gone over so far. This helped me a lot. Starting off with writing down what I spent my day doing. Crossing off what are the things I could be spending less time on or completely delete from my daily schedule. Then write down things I wanted to accomplish, both big and small. Lastly I wrote down what things I could do little by little to be a step closer to accomplishing those goals. You can write it as a list, or make little rows and columns, whatever floats your beautiful boat. Don't feel lame having a "dream journal", cause lets be real this is exactly what we're making. I'm sure the lame dream journal holders have probably been the most powerful and influential people in the world. So I say it doesn't hurt to give it a try.

Chapter 4

You

Now that we've created our little dream journal and feel empowered lets completely move on to a different subject. With great power and super power comes great responsibility and cautious behavior. As we see in the media and in our daily lives at work and school, people's behavior affects the reaction to their works. Lets say the great Ms. J.K Rowling, despite the fact that her Harry Potter series is one of the most brilliant and amazing works ever seen in our time, we later find out she's totally arrogant, ignorant, racist, obnoxious, selfish and just the most horrible person you have ever met. Ugh, I can't even fathom that scenario.

Well let's say that were the case, what would happen to all the Harry Potter stuff? I know people would probably see it in a different light. Not because its not good, but because by buying her books you are supporting her and if we support her its like we agree with her ideals and behavior. I'm sure there would be a few "unique" individuals who probably would buy her stuff even more, but lets not talk about them. Thankfully that is not the case. J.K Rowling is a talented, amazing, powerful woman who is respected and loved by millions and shares humane ideals and a humble personality. I've never met her but I'm certain I'm right in my assumptions.

Think about you. Does your personality and ideals fit with

what you're trying to accomplish? Will it target the people you want? Does your behavior reflect what you believe? I can share with you by own personal experience. My personality is very….uhh….hmm…what was the question again? Oh right! I'm not sure what kind of personality I have. I've taken too many personality tests and read personality books and I'm still not 100% confident in what I am. If that's you too, don't feel bad. I'm here for you. I do know this; I know that I'm very caring; I can be funny when I'm comfortable enough. I can talk a lot if I'm with the right person. I'm also sensitive and like to be in charge, but not all the time. Most importantly, I dislike being dishonest and dishonest people, and I live by the saying "what goes around comes around".

So I do my best to be the most honest and kind person I can be. That's really what it all comes down to. You don't necessarily have to know what personality type you are. You just need to learn what your values are. Then you need to learn to be kind, first to yourself and then to others, Learn to love, again first you and then everyone, regardless whether they share the same values as you or not. Learn to be patient, with you then everyone and learn to be honest with you and then everyone. If you don't treat yourself right, Karma will come back to you. When YOU don't put YOU first (after whatever greater power you believe in), that's when the problems start. You get sad, depressed, unmotivated. You start to feel unworthy and doubt your efforts. You start to sink into a deep hole of self-hate and self-doubt.

If that's the case then, STOP it. First of all, take a breather; think about five things you like about yourself. If you cant think of all five that's ok. One is good enough. Now take those things and focus on them during your day. If you like that you're patient, note down the times you were patient with someone. If you like that you know how to cook really good deliciousness then maybe cook something for someone and write down what their reaction was in receiving it. Right there, you just added another thing to your list, you are kind and generous, that's two more!

But, isn't it a little selfish to put yourself first? Maybe you're a full time mom (hardest job in the world by the way, props to all the moms) and you don't even have time to take your morning poop in peace, that's ok! You can put yourself first for even a few seconds. It doesn't have to be a whole day thing and you don't have to completely stop doing things for others just because you want to focus on you. Trust me, the minute you stop thinking about everyone else but yourself for **too long**, it'll make you feel depressed and defeat the purpose of this chapter. So what do you do then? You become patient, with you. What does that even mean? You know how there are times when we are super overwhelmed by an annoying customer or co-worker, and most of all our children and people we live with?! This is the time when you back up for a second. Take a deep breath and give yourself some props for doing a good job. Tell yourself you're a beautiful beast who knows yelling at that lady wont make her go away or smacking your kids wont get them to stop crying. Then come back to reality and even if you don't have a solution you'll know you're a better person for not losing it and will deal with it like a queen OR king.

When you do something kind of tempting, like waste the whole day binge watching *Orange Is The New Black* on Netflix when you told yourself you would use the day to clean out your room, don't feel defeated. I mean you watched 200 40-minute episodes, that's got to be some kind of record, right? Take a breath and commit to yourself you'll get it done that week. Trust me, we all accidently binge watch something once in a while.

If you have self hate issues, stop that right now. I'm no therapist but why do you hate yourself so much? Did you do something wrong? Unless you killed your neighbor's dog or another human being on purpose (murderer), I think you need to take a beat and listen to me for a minute.

IF you really have an issue where you feel helpless and want to give up and you see no remedy and the only way out is if you disappear from this earth, please, please, please for you and those who love you, seek professional help. That's why people become therapist, to help people who feel that way. Usually a lot of them have been there and done that and know exactly how to help. If you don't like the ones you've listened to then find a new one. Just don't give up on yourself, please. Trust me, I know what its like to feel alone and unhappy and not even know the reason and feel guilty for feeling that way, especially when you have people who love and support you. It's a very horrible and frustrating type of emotional pain and desperation when all you want to do is stop being a burden to yourself and others. I know, and I'm here to tell you you're not alone, and you're not done with life and you're definitely not a burden. You belong here and you have a calling to fulfill and you're the only one that can do it. You are not a mistake or a waste of life. There is no such thing or person who was brought to this earth by accident. If you're here its because you have a job to do. People to nspire, no matter how few or many. People to love and care for, and there are people who love and care for you. This dark hole you feel stuck in is temporary and you and everyone around you has the power to get you out of it. Its not forever, I promise. Also, you got to see what happens when they remake all the live action movies into animation! That's going to be something cool to watch. Hang in there, the world needs you here. You need you here. I need you here.

There is this quote from the TV show called Sherlock Holmes, and even though it's a fantasy world, this quote is very relevant and very real; "Taking you own life. Interesting expression — taking it from who? Once it's over, it's not you who'll miss it. Your own death is something that happens to everybody else. Your life is not your own. Keep your hands off it."

If you're like me and have a feature of yourself you wish you didn't have, then fix it. Not by getting surgery, or filtering the heck out of your face. Learn to embrace it. I have always been very insecure about my weight. I've looked at celebrities and other people and wished I could look like them. Even when I did lose weight and felt ok with myself, I still wasn't good enough. So I learned that it didn't matter if I was 150 or

200 lbs., we see ourselves flawed because we don't love ourselves enough to see our beauty.

I see all these models that are unique and different from what the "conventional" model is supposed to look like and it's amazing! When I see these people I realize that they have embraced what society would call a "flaw" and used it to become role models and leaders to people who are just like them. To show the world that the only flaw in an ugly personality. So, embrace yourself and use that beautiful "flaw" to inspire others and help them learn to love themselves just like you did.

Now that I feel like I've blabbed so much and this chapter was all over the place (like all the other ones), lets write some stuff down!

First, write down some things you love/loved about yourself. If you cant think of anything ask someone you trust to help you. If its something you "loved" write down why you don't anymore. What can you do to bring that back?

Second, write down the words *kindness, charity, patience, love* and *honesty*. Then during the week keep tabs on which ones you've shown and how many times you showed each of these to yourself and others. Try to experiment with it. See what happens when you start off your day focusing on you

first (even if you have to get up before the kids do) see how
that affects you day and how you treat others.

You bored yet? Hope not! Cause I'm just getting started!

Chapter 5

No Good Deed

My husband and I are huge musical fans. Ok not **huge**, we've seen *Wicked* two times *The Lion King Musical* once and *Frozen* like five times (I count that as a musical, don't judge me). But we enjoy them a lot and hope to see more soon, once I sell millions of copies of my books and can buy us some tickets. Anyway, there's a song in *Wicked* where she says, "No good deed goes unpunished. No act of charity goes unresented." This is the truest thing I've ever heard in my English speaking life and it's also in my "quotes to live by" file. Once we start getting in the grind of living positively and doing good for ourselves and others, there's a relapse moment. Some time or other we will bump into someone or something that makes our efforts seem unappreciated or unseen.

For example, let's say you have been working on serving others. You have taken the time to make a cake for someone or helping a friend walk their dog every week. Maybe you've been helping your little sibling with their math homework every night. Then one day the universe decides to roll over on its back and the inevitable happens. That last cake you made gave your friend major poops, the dog saw a cat and you lost grip of the leash and it got hurt in the process, and your little sis or bro came back furious because they got a D on their math test. Of course everyone is going to blame whom? Yep, you. So what do you do now?

In times like this our automatic reaction is usually to break down and tell ourselves "that's the last time I'm doing that." and the only reason we do that is because we let fear in. I imagine our bodies like a machine with a bunch of little tanks for every emotion. When we are doing what makes us happy and serving other people our love and happy tank are full and the ones who are running the show. When everything goes wrong and we "failed" then fear, anxiety, anger and sadness take over. Kind of like that movie *Inside Out.* If you have never watched that movie and are wondering what the heck I'm talking about then put this book down right now, go ask someone if you can borrow it or rent it and watch it! Don't read anything again until you've watched that movie. Its a Pixar movie, who doesn't watch a Pixar movie? Cold-hearted sociopaths? I don't know.

Anyway, When this happens we have a few options, we can either let all those negative emotions take over 100% and never let them go and live a salty lonely life OR we cry for a few, get up, say sorry and keep on the good deeds. If the person doesn't want or need your help anymore then that's ok. Don't ever let a situation like that affect your relationships with anyone. Being your best self is being humble and not taking things too personal or getting angry at someone for not wanting you around so much.

Don't be salty and tell them you'll never bake a cake for them ever again or tell your little brother you hope he fails all his tests. That's just setting yourself up for more despair. Be confident that you did your best and do good no matter what the outcome is. There is no greater joy than to do good deeds for others and that helps you love and appreciate yourself more than you can ever possibly imagine.

One real life example I can think of is my dad. He is a small business owner who has seen and worked with all kinds of people in the 20+ years he's been doing this. I vaguely remember one person he helped who worked with him. My dad was opening another business in another city that's about an hour and half away from where we lived. He was starting from zero so he had no one who lived out there that he knew. This guy who worked with him at his current business offered to go and work. My dad said yeah and he offered to buy a house so he can rent it, my dads always going the extra mile to help others. Anywho, this guy goes and takes his family, has a place to live, a job and despite that those things were the act of a good deed, he complained and complained. He eventually blamed my dad for moving him there (even though the guy offered) and within no time he stopped paying rent, causing my dad to lose the house and eventually due to not being able to find someone who was willing to manage the store, he sold it.

I cant even tell you how many more times my dad helped someone with this big gesture and how many more times those he helped used that gesture to screw him over. Its unbelievable what some people will do. Its even more unbelievable how many people don't own up to their own mistakes. Its like if I gave Bob a car so he can show up to work on time and I'm paying for it because he cant afford it and really needs this job. Then one day bob needs to get an oil change but doesn't do it cause he's not paying for the car. The car breaks down and doesn't work, who is Bob going to blame? Himself for not being responsible human being and maintain the car he's driving to work every day? Or me for giving him a "bad car". Trust me guys, I've seen so many messed up things in this world. But the one thing that's most relatable, messed up and likely to happen to anyone is someone taking advantage of their kindness.

With all that said, my dad is still the most generous and caring person I know. He of course gets upset at some people and has a limit to how much abuse he can handle. He eventually stops helping that particular person or helps them one more time with whatever he can and shows them how to vent for themselves with the hopes that they listen. Of course people will kick and scream the minute you stop helping them. Still my father has one of the kindest hearts and is one of the most humble people I know. Despite what he's been though he doesn't hold resentment. He continues to help where he sees help is needed.

Don't let unfortunate events like the ones I mentioned change your heart. Learn from them; think about how you can be more careful next time and what you can do different so your help is more effective. The last thing you want to do is hold grudges and declare you'll never do a good deed ever again. You'll just turn your heart into a black piece of coal. Its in our nature to help others, just like it is to survive. We need to bring that part of ourselves out and put it to work. By doing that, only then will we start seeing some progress in our lives and in this world. One good deed a day, even a week can make a huge huge huge difference.

Now, for the writing part. Take that handy dandy notebook you've been using and write down good deeds you have worked on, are working on and will work on. For each write down the good and the ugly. Have you ever done something good for someone and it didn't pan out the way you hoped? Is it something you can try again? If so, will you? Write down what are some things you can do during the week, month and year. Starting with small deeds and work your way up to big, more time consuming ones. Trust me, this will change the way you see yourself and your fellow humans. No happy life is complete without serving others.

Chapter 6

Patience

We all know the saying "patience is a virtue" and most of us learn this when we are waiting for our happy meal at McDonalds and our moms tell us to be patient. This is true, but a lot of children and truthfully some adults don't even know what the heck virtue means. So what is virtue? Well if you look it up on Google you will learn that it means to be an honorable person. Someone who is respectable, good, pure. Pretty much someone who has no bad intentions. So what does patience have to do with being good and honorable? Who knows? I wish I had a legitimate answer for that. I can however give you my point of view.

Take every single successful and happy person in the world. Not someone who processes just one of those traits, the people who have both, success and happiness. Who did they sleep with to get there? No one! Well that's true for MOST, I'm sure there's a few sleepy peeps in there. Most people who have success and happiness are those who worked hard and then... waited. Worked hard again and waited again. Then finally when the world would tell them to give up, they worked three times harder, waited and boom!

Success doesn't mean becoming, rich and famous, it means to be in a place where you are proud with what you've done and are living a great life that you are grateful with. For the sake of giving an example everyone can understand I will use celebrities and influential people. Lets start with actors and musicians. I know a lot of people in the world dislike celebrities who became famous just by being born into an already rich and famous family, but with most actors and musicians its different, people usually like them more than heirs and heiresses or reality show people, and for the most part its because musicians and actors are the most relatable.

Madonna didn't come out of the womb with 7 Grammys, the Marvel Cinematic Universe (MCU) and all its cast and crew didn't one day just say "Hey guys, you know what would be cool? If we all got together and made a bunch of super hero movies." Leonardo DiCaprio didn't happen to walk by James Cameron and say "Hey can I be in your movie? I'm really good at pretending to be frozen." If things were that easy, I would have gone to Disney Studios and asked to became the face of all things Disney, especially the MCU.... sorry Mickey and Iron man.

All these people are relatable to us because they worked their butts off to get to where they are in these hard times. If you hear all their stories of their first movies or gigs, you'd probably think they were lying. Some of them struggled with illnesses and addictions, some of them lost loved ones, some of them were homeless and more broke than you and I will ever be. Regardless of what adversities came their way they worked like no one else, hours upon hours with little sleep and lots of time away from loved ones to be able to create a legacy. For some it might sound selfish to be away from those you love to pursue a career such as these. But when you have a dream to be an actor or singer, the timing is right and you find people who love you and respect your dream then its not that big of a problem. So I have always felt a sense of proudness towards those types of celebrities. Especially now that I follow some of them on social media and see the long hours they work and all they give back. They definitely earned the luxurious life they live.

An example of success without fame is, well…. everybody else. Doctors, educators, honest lawyers, producers, construction workers, plumbers, receptionist, mothers, fathers, etc. When you find a path you love and are great at, that you do with integrity and love, that can help you grow and support your family, gives you the means and ability to give back and are able to teach and pass valuable knowledge down to others, to me that's success. It takes just as much energy and determination to achieve any profession and milestone in life. I admire people who work, study and come home to attend to their families every single day. Ill be the first to admit that it takes a lot of patience, love, discipline and balance to pull that off. You have to divide your time between each one so you can give them 100% of you. So even if there's 100 things you want to do, don't think about doing them all at once. Take your time with each one so you're able to be the best employee, student, spouse, friend and parent you can be.

Whether you're already super famous and wealthy or working your dream job, there might something that you would want achieve next or maybe you can mentor those who need a little push. For those of us who still haven't found our calling in life or are waiting for the universe to move the sun and stars so we can wake up in our dream land, lets take a step back to reality. Things wont come if we don't work for them and even after we work for them, we wont get to the highest point with one try. Success takes time, for some more than others and that's OK. Life is not a competition or about what you deserve, no one deserves anything, yet, everyone deserves everything. Just by being the kindest most generous person in the world doesn't mean you deserve any kind of compensation. 12th place trophies don't exist and they shouldn't, cause then what's the point of trying to be the best when you can be mediocre and get recognition? That way of thinking is just a recipe for disaster. Your **works** will get you the things you **earn**. When you work hard, maybe even struggle a bit in a dead end job or with horrible co workers, if you pull though long enough, have been the best person you can be and followed the golden rule, then opportunities will rise.

If you keep job hopping because your jobs keep getting harder, you've become impatient with your co-workers or you're just bored, then more than likely you'll probably be on the same boat for a long time. Understand that if you want to get paid more, you're gonna have to work more. CEOs got to where they are by working their brain down so much they need people to do the work for them and when the next person earns their comfy seat and high pay with less work, it will come. (Disclaimer: less work usually means more responsibilities over others and maybe a little more stress, which is fine -if you got what it takes.). If you can't wait that long then you can start your own business. Again, this will take a lot of time and effort especially if you're starting from zero. BE PATIENT. It will take a few years to get to where you want to be, but if you keep starting over because you don't want to work harder then you will never get there.

So lets get down to business…. to defeat…THE HUNS! Sorry, I don't know how to complete that sentence any other way. Ok, time for keeping track of what we are doing. Lets start with writing down some things we feel impatient about and think of solutions or things we can do to take it one step at a time and be more patient. Whatever it may be, maybe you're impatient with your kids best friend who keeps coming over and eating your food. You can try to talk to them and see how their day has been, get to know them better. Maybe their mom doesn't cook for them, or they have a black hole in their stomach, you never know. But if you have been applying the things I've talked about so far you know that service, love and good karma is key. If you feel like you're just not getting an closer to your goals, write down things that might be keeping them from happening or things you can do different to get there a little bit faster.

If you are impatient with yourself for any reason, write down why. Always write down why when it comes to you. Its harder to evaluate your feelings for yourself if you don't put it into perspective. Others see you in a different light, so when you're frustrated with you, write it down. If you're frustrated because you could have done better on that test, or maybe you yelled at your spouse or child and realize you could have handled that differently, write down what you can do to make amends and avoid doing it again. There is also the possibility that you have become impatient with yourself because you aren't really doing anything to better your situation, don't worry. Opportunities will come if we keep pushing forward. Time moves with or without us, so don't forget to do your best to use each day wisely to keep moving closer to a better more fulfilling life.

Remember what I said about putting yourself first? Well, if you cant be patient with your self how the heck are you going to find patience for somebody else? Can I get a amen? (did that make you think of RuPaul? I hope so!) Don't be so hard on yourself. Its ok, we all make mistakes, we all lag it sometimes and we all lose our cool every once in a while. Especially now a days with all that's going on in the world. Take a good look at yourself, on paper, and work on the things you need to take it a little more easy with and focus on what you have control over. We will live a long life of misery if we keep getting frustrated and upset over things that have already happened or that we have no power over. Focus on what you can change about you to be that kind, patient, tolerant person you wish to be and it will become easier to be patient and tolerant with others.

Chapter 7

Treal yo' Self.

I don't know how many times I've re-watched shows on Netflix. There's usually an order and its *The Office, How I met Your Mother* and *Parks and Recreation.* I can't say I have a favorite from those three…wait, yes I can, its *The Office.* Anyway, each one has their own little charm to it and things I can relate to and things that I find inspirational. One of my favorite things about the third show are two characters who every year they have a day called "treat yo' self-day". The day usually starts off with one of them sending the other an extravagant message, usually containing music and a cake with the words "treat yo' self." The two spend the day treating themselves to luxuries and items they wouldn't buy otherwise. They each encouraged the other into buying whatever they fancied. I wish it were a real holiday, wonder how we can make that happen….hmm.

My favorite 'treat yo self' episode is the one when they invite a third friend who happens to be a bit nerdy and uptight. Because he was having really bad day, they decide to bring him along on their day of pampering and shopping. He was not enjoying any of the activities and apologizes to them for ruining the day. Towards the end of the day one of them is frustrated with him because while they all bought very expensive and fancy items, he just bought socks.

Acknowledging that maybe that was his version of a "treat" he was asked "If you could blow big money on one thing, what would it be?". In the next scene we see him in a Batman costume and his friends are shocked and amused.

My favorite thing about this episode is that in the end they recognized that not every ones version of luxuries or rewards is the same. For example, maybe someone likes to go hike up a mountain for fun and look at the landscape. Some people like to go to theme parks, others like to stay at home and watch a movie, and of course you have the ones who do like to spend a lot of money on something they really want and makes them feel good and fancy. All of those are very valid and none of them makes someone vain or selfish. Its ok to be a little flashy sometimes and its also ok if you find the same amount of joy sitting at home with your dog. The point is to find what that "treat" is and work for it and to maybe check how we spend our time and turn something we might do everyday and take for granted into a "treat".

Usually a treat is something a dog gets when its being rewarded for good behavior. Well, it's not just for the dogs. Through hard work and obedience, we find the way to change our bad habits and create a better lifestyle and eventually find the means to treat ourselves. Whether it's about saving money or saving time, with either being very doable, it still takes patience, lots of determination and obedience.

So let's talk about some ways we can treat ourselves and how we could get there. Let's say you really want to take a trip to Disneyland, like me! Even though I've been there so many times, the number of times I need to go to get tired of this place does not exit. "The limit does not exist!" I love *Mean Girls.* Anyway, You need time and money! So one thing I started doing was stop spending unnecessary cash during the week and put it into my little savings. Some examples included buying fast food, buying junk food, buying stuff I didn't need and of course buying more fast food. Because I spent so much money eating fast food or snacks, I got into the habit of setting a grocery budget and stuck to it. Because its only my husband and I its not very hard to keep it under $200 a month.

What does make it hard is those unexpected long days where we get too hungry to go home and cook something and spend our date budget on In N Out. Despite those little trips, it works and I do count eating out as a reward of some kind because I don't do it as often anymore. I may not have hundreds of dollars saved up yet, but every little bit counts. This is where the patience and determination comes in and I either work harder to get there faster, sit there and freak out about not having more money or relax before I have a heart attack and die and end up not making more.

My husbands' idea of a treat is very dependent on his mood. One day he could tell me he'll be fine having a day when he comes home and all we do is enjoy each others company, eat a home cooked meal and watch Marvel movies. On other days his perfect 'treat yo' self' day would be a trip to his homeland, Dominican Republic (which we haven't done, yet). So it's a little difficult to know which one to shoot for, so I tend to focus on the former first and work our way up.

Before moving to Utah he had a very intense schedule; He would be up at 3am, commute 2 hours to work and would get home until 7 or 8 in the evening, eat real quick and go to bed. It was horrible. Lots of people in California live that way, not everyone but most of the people we knew in our town commuted to Los Angeles for work. Now he only commutes 8 minutes to work and is home before 4! We have most of the day together and are able to have more quality time than ever before. So we are able to get his first, easier "treat yo self" day marked off.

Any kind of reward requires some sort of sacrifice.

Whether we need to take time off from one thing to give to the other or stop spending so much on coffee every morning and get in the habit of brewing your own. It's a little exhausting at times but its well worth it. Again, don't feel bad for taking a day to give yourself what you want once in a while. I'm not saying go blow up money at the mall every week, or take an expensive trip every month because you decided to "treat yourself".

What I am saying is that it's ok if maybe once a year or every 6 months you want to take a trip with your loved one, away from the kids for a few days. You're not bad parents for wanting to spend some time away from them, they're people and no matter how much we love them we get tired of people eventually and need some space. Maybe you are super into fitness but you also want to go watch a movie with friends or spend some extra time with your dog. Missing a gym day every other week wont make you lose all the progress you've made.

Again, just to clarify, I'm not saying to call in sick to work or miss your class because you decided to go do whatever you wanted. Use common sense and figure out ways you can "treat yo' self" every now and then. Also, don't make a habit out of it because then it's not a treat and you're just living a luxury you may not be able to afford. Look at your daily schedule and figure what is something you can "sacrifice" for a bit so you can give yourself that reward in a few months or weeks. Think about how often you want to do that? If its something that cost a lot, like a trip, then maybe try to do it once every two years or if your budget allows it then once every year. If it's something that requires giving up time you can do it maybe once a month or every few months. As long as you feel comfortable with it and it wont sabotage your means of income, your relationships and progression, then go for it!

P.S. As a millennial who grew up in a country like the Unites States, I recognize that there are a lot of things we all take for granted. I share this just to put things into perspective. My husband, who grew up in the Dominican Republic and was born only three weeks before me, had a completely different upbringing than I did. He tells me stories like how they only had pizza on Christmas because it was a special treat for them, and very expensive. So every Christmas they looked forward to the pizza that, by the way, was home made! I feel like an ungrateful punk whenever I think about how my parents bought us pizza all the time. I never saw it as a treat, I saw it as dinner. He also told me of a time his younger brother got a can of Pringles for his birthday and he was so exited. He shared it with everyone at his party, and it wasn't the big can you get at the dollar store, it was the little travel size you put into your kids lunch box.

I know all our parents wanted (and I think this is true for most of our parents) was to give us everything they never had. This is probably why we take things for granted, we never got to really struggle because they were able to buy us things and take us places, which I know we are all extremely grateful for. For the most part they worked their butts off so we didn't have to. They might have unintentionally raised us to take certain things for granted and maybe kept us from learning some valuable lessons. I know we live in a time where we can buy a can of Pringles for $1 or a $5 pizza, and that's great. However, we still need to be appreciative and teach the younger generations that owning the latest gadgets isn't a right or something they have to have or deserve, its a privilege and reward for being great kids.

Chapter 8

Learn and Lead

This generation is in a very tricky spot. The older generations hate us or dislikes us (even though they raised us) because they feel we are incompetent due to the fact that we try to find the easiest way to do things and that's most likely due to all the technology we have access to and its ability to make all things available and convenient. The younger generations seem to be lacking common sense and social awareness because they are the first generation to not have lived in a world with no smart phones and social networks; It's crazy to think about. Also, they are the generation WE are raising.

We need to be cautious to not take away ALL of the struggle and inconvenience from them, a little struggle will help them learn appreciation, work ethic and a few other things. So how do we get the older generation off our backs and the younger ones to leave their cold and aloof zombie ways and help them better the world and themselves? You gather all the possible resources you can and get to learnin'.

One of the things I have seen and the reason why I was inspired to write this book is the number of people who are in their 40s, 50s and even 60s that are just now finding ways to get out of their current situation at work or at home, to live a better life, but why? It's usually because they sought help too late, usually out of fear of failing and getting out of their comfort zone. So I'm here to tell all my peers who are just getting started with figuring out adulthood and real life to get off your Snapchat and Facebook because the answers are not there, and go to Barnes and Noble and look for the self development section and check a book out. You can even YouTube and look up leadership or inspirational talks from world-class leaders and speakers who have it all figured out. Don't listen to your friend who is on the same boat as you and convinces you that "it is what is." That's probably the worst thing anyone can say ever!

The truth of the matter is that it is NOT what it is. The people telling you that are in the position they are in and living that life you don't want because that's how *they* think. They may seem happy and probably are, but you don't want their life, still you listen to them just because they seem happy. Fast Forward 20 years and you're on the same boat as that person only you didn't want what they had. So what happened? You listened to the wrong guy! Look for someone who inspires you and who has the type of lifestyle you eventually want to live. If it's someone who is either not alive anymore or out of reach, then read books about them or follow them on social media sites. Learn how they thought/think and what they did/do. Even if it sounds insane or too good to be true.

I once went to an open meeting for a company that focuses on helping people learn financial literacy and personal development skills, and one of the speakers made a great point. She said "Crazy people get crazy results." and she's right. When you decide to start learning and thinking out of the box whether its going back to school to take a random class on mechanics after working the same office job for 15 years or start attending a new church that has made you feel inspired to become a better person or simply started setting a schedule or to-do list for yourself to be more productive, or writing a book…go for it! Know that it may take time, ruffle some feathers and people will start calling you crazy or tell you to get your head out of the clouds, ignore them.

When you do decide to learn new things to become more self-aware and self-sufficient don't let it get in the way of your work, church or family. Those things are crucial to give you that extra support you may need, even if they think what you're doing is too crazy to work, or too good to be true. When you have a group of people that loves you, they will support you as long as they see progress and change in you. Unless they're at a point in their lives that you aspire to be, I suggest you don't take their comments too seriously. Find yourself a mentor and fill your head and heart with positive and motivational comments and ideas.

After we listen to all of the mentors and teachers we can find, it's time for us to pay it forward. It's a little selfish to have all this knowledge of how to live an awesome life and not share it. So that's when you get to work. How? Living by example, that's how. You may not know this but there are quite a few people who are watching you very closely. They either look up to you or are curious to see where life takes you and its your job to show both of these people how to live like a champ. You become their inspiration and they follow you, just like you followed those who taught you.

Think about your job, who's in charge? Think about whether that person is a boss or a leader. If you don't know the difference between someone who bosses people around and someone who leads them, or you think they're the same thing then maybe you're the bossy one, so reevaluate yo'self. A boss is someone who tells people what to do and expects the person they told to know what they are doing and the boss doesn't really move a finger. For example, I'm in my office and call Sarah, who's been working with me for a few days. I tell her to go clean the chairs in the dining area and send a fax to a client. She goes and does what I told her. The next day I call her into my office and scold her because the legs of the chairs were dirty and she sent the fax to the wrong client. So how in the heck was Sarah supposed to know what I was asking of her?

A leader would take Sarah and show her how to properly clean the chairs and tell her the client number and possibly even show her how to send a fax. A leader teaches and a boss just spits out demands that they're not even able to do. That's the difference. When you are able to lead, your work and home become a place where people feel accomplished and capable. Just because you may have all this knowledge or have worked at a place for many years, doesn't give you any kind of merit that says you're better than someone else or are allowed to make them feel inferior. Again, that's a boss not a leader.

Leading and teaching by example is the most effective way to get someone to learn the things you want them to and to progress and move on to the next step. In school, teachers didn't just say "draw the letter A" to a bunch of 5 years olds and assume they all knew it and not bother to show them on the board how to write it. Life doesn't work like that. Just like we each individually learned from others growing up, whether it was from watching someone in real life or reading a book, people cant learn to lead if there's no one around to show them. So be the leader and mentor someone. If everyone on this earth would take the time to learn new principles to help them become better people and taught someone to do the same, we'd be unstoppable. I don't even know what a world of leaders would look like. Not politicians or dictators, but leaders. It's fun to think about, it's also not impossible. We just need to have an ambition, follow it, learn it and teach it.

Now it's that time again. Bring out that notebook or piece of paper you've been taking notes with. Think of someone you admire, or someone you might have heard of that has done great things in this world and you look up to. Set a goal for the week or month to check out a book on self-development. This can be about anything you might want to enhance in your life; love and relationships, finances, work ethic, patience, etc. I have not read it yet but I heard *7 Habits of Highly Effective People* is a great book. Personality *plus, 5 love languages* all highly recommended. Those two books changed my life and have made my husband and me better people to each other and to those around us. Also look up YouTube videos, TED talks are great. While you're doing those things, make sure you are applying what you learn. If you don't do the homework how do you expect to pass the class? There will be little to no change in you or your life if you don't apply the principles you are learning. So make sure you do that or else it doesn't work and you'll be wasting your time. Also, don't forget to write down any changes you see, whether it's in yourself or the way others are treating you.

Once you've become the master of awesomeness, and have learned something worth sharing make a list of people who might benefit from what you're learning. This right here is also an act of service. Remember way back when I said without serving others there's really no glory or point to any of this? Well, here is where you can factor that in. Once you have your list, call or text them and say, "Hey, I've been reading this book and its completely changed my perspective of things, you should really check it out. I think you'll really like it." and boom, you've done your part of helping a friend be a better them.

People will always notice when something is different about you, whether its good or bad. So make sure that's its good and do the best you can to be a great example of what a good human being looks like. Become a leader, first in your own life and eventually you will find yourself leading others into a life full of opportunities none of you ever imagined.

P.S. When finding people to learn from make sure you are diverse in who you pick. Don't pick a friend who may have excellent finances to learn about love or marriage. It doesn't have to be one person who you think has all the qualities you want just because they have ONE. Find a happy couple to learn about relationships. Find someone who's living financially secure to learn about finances. You can have more than one awesome friend who has something admirable about them (If you don't, then go out and make one). Always take the best qualities and habits from different people and try to apply them to yourself.

Chapter 9

Spread it out.

This will probably be the shortest chapter you will ever read (not really) and its all about spreading it out! I don't know what comes to mind when you think of spreading it out, but I'll just tell you what I mean. Do the following to or with others; smile, embrace, wave, converse, make eye-contact, shake hands, acknowledge, advise, listen, care, heal, sympathize, laugh, love. I cannot stress enough how important it is that we get out of our narcissistic ways, drop the phone for a minute and realize that life is not in these little gadgets we cling onto so much. Yes, social media and all this technology is great and we should use it to its fullest potential, but not to dismiss those around us or to show the world our filtered lives just to disappoint ourselves.

We need to remember that there's I don't know how many billion more people on this earth, and hundreds even thousands that we share our life with, at the store, at the movies, at school, work and of course at home. Each and every one of them makes up our life. Without any of them we would be completely alone and with no purpose. Next time you go to Trader Joes or a Vallarta Supermarket, smile at the cashier, even if they don't smile back. Give a nod to someone and acknowledge their presence. Introduce yourself and shake some ones hand if you started a conversation. Make sure you say bye to that person you were conversing in line with before you leave, and wish them a good day. We really don't know what kind of positive effect any of these actions might have on someone. Every single person on this planet is going through something. However big or small the adversity might be, it's there.

So, even a smile or a nod can send a positive message to someone and change the outcome of their whole day for the better. Also if you know of someone who can use the information you have gained throughout this book and any other resource, share it! If your in-laws are going through some financial crisis and you just learned about the 47 principles of financial fitness or now know what financial literacy is, share it! If your friend and her significant other are going through a rough patch and you have read books on relationships that have helped you, share it! If you did something that's changed your life for the better in any way, share it! You cant find a candy bar and keep it all to yourself. You'll break out or grow an extra chin because you didn't share. Greed is one of the most evil things that exist in this world and it comes in many forms. So get out there and spread the love and knowledge. Do a service to others by doing any of the things I've mentioned in this chapter. It will definitely help you as well.

Chapter 10

Own it

You've finally reached the end of reading all the nonsense had to say. In this last chapter I want to make sure you understood what the whole point of reading this book was and whether or not you're applying the advice I've given. I'll be honest, I hardly ever remember what a book says cover to cover, and it's usually the main points or maybe some juicy tea that was spilled throughout book. But since this one had no good tea (by 'tea' or "T" I mean gossip) and my points were probably all over the place, Ill sum it down for you.

The first thing you need to do as soon as you're done reading this book is turn off your TV, exit your social media app, probably turn off the news for a minute and go to Barnes and Noble. You're going to buy yourself a notebook or journal, some nice pens (you can probably get this at the dollar store or something), and buy one or two books on personal development. These books can be about ANYTHING that has to do with enhancing yourself as a person professionally, financially, socially or personally. Read them, most books are not that long and a lot of them give you the highlights at the end or have little workbooks that come with it to make it easier. If you're definitely not a reader then look for audios or videos. As I mentioned before there is an infinite amount of resources on the Internet. I know you guys know your way around the World Wide Web, so it should not be difficult to Google or YouTube a few talks.

Next, you're going to get yourself a little poster board or bulletin board and create what some people like to call a "dream board". I know, I know that's so cheesy, right? Well, don't forget trying not to be cheesy isn't working for you, I mentioned that earlier too. So get over yourself. Once you have your poster or whatever you bought, look up pictures that represent your dreams. Don't forget to dream BIG! No matter your age or where you live, dream. Even the impossible can be possible. Take into considerations all aspects of your life. Where do you want to be financially? How do you want your family dynamic to be? Who do you want to inspire? What can you do to get there? Who can help you? Where do you want to travel? What do you want be? What does your dream house look like? Your car? How many dogs or kids do you want to have? The questions are endless.

Once you have your dream board it's time to do one better thing a day. No matter what it is. You can wake up earlier so you can do your bed before you leave your house. You can prepare your meal a day before so you're not tempted to eat out and spend more money. You can say 'hi' to someone you see everyday and usually don't say hi to. You can go to work with the mind set that its a stepping stone or an opportunity to learn and grow and prepare yourself for the next big thing and if you love your job, show it! Take your spouse on a date; surprise them with something they like. Ladies, this isn't just a guy job to come home with flowers and chocolates, we need to pamper and make the men feel appreciated too. Believe it or not they have feelings, some of them are way deep down in their gut but they are there. Take your dog on a walk or set aside 5 minutes to teach them that trick or behavior you want them to learn. Trust me, you will be so glad you taught Scribbles how to sit still when she's inside. There are so many things we don't think about that we can do to make our lives just a little bit more blissful.

Of course, you must always focus on you first (even for a second) before you try to focus on someone else. You cant feed your family if you're not feeding yourself. You can't teach someone how to be friendly if you're not friendly, and you definitely can't love someone if you don't love you. This is crucial to living the life you want and being the person you want to be. Remember when I told you to turn off your TV? Well you turn off all the haters too. People, even sometimes those closest to you will unfortunately try to damage you. I don't know why, but that's just the way the world is. Not everyone has those people in their lives, but a lot of us do. So even if it's someone you cant really delete from your life, ignore them, or embrace their hate and turn into motivation to prove them wrong and show them what a bad a** you are.

Next come the good deeds and the patience. This is where I feel the world, especially the younger generations, need to work on. I know most people are good and have good intentions. However, most people don't have the initiative to act upon that goodness or use it to better someone else's life. A lot of us are shy or feel incompetent. Well, if you've been doing the one thing different a day and got rid of some of that shyness, then it's time to get to the deeds. Good deeds are not just giving money to the homeless, its any kind of service. A smile, helping someone with their work, being there to comfort a friend, helping your parents by washing their car or picking up the dog poop. It can even be a phone call to your grandma that you haven't spoken to in months. Big deeds like charity work are important of course and we need them to make a difference in the world, but all these small deeds are what you need to make a difference in your life and the life of those around you.

Of course with all these good deeds you may stumble upon some that backfire and this is where you need lots and ots of patience and tolerance. I know that working on yourself can be hard and you want to see a difference in your life tomorrow. Well, you and I both know that's not going to happen. EVERYTHING in this life takes patience, love and nurturing. Your job, family, friends, and yourself all take time to become better. As I mentioned earlier in the book, Madonna wasn't built in one day. You will have your whole life to build yourself. Even if you're halfway through life, you're not done. This is why I have you build a dream board so you know where you want to be at a certain point in your life. I know I probably wont want be having babies when I'm 50, so that's a goal for my 30s. I probably want to spend the rest of my days living at a beach house in Dominican Republic, but that's not until I'm in my 60s. It's all about perspective and making sure that you are aware that big picture goals are not just a one-time thing. It can be many things at different points in your life. So be patient and keep on doing your homework.

After you have put in the work and have been able to make some time or save some extra money, then its time to reward yourself. Remember that you rewarding yourself doesn't always have to be spending all your savings on a trip to the Disney store or taking a fancy vacation. Start with little things like watching movie at home and ordering pizza, or going on a walk or taking a nap. If you have to spend some money make sure you're still cautious and be smart about it. You can go to the movies or get some ice cream. Remember the harder you work the bigger the reward can be. If you do end up taking a trip then it will probably be after you've saved up enough money and time to go take it. Only you know what you're working towards and how much work you're willing to put in.

Last but not least, educate yourself and share your knowledge. I'm not talking about your college education; I'm talking about your real life education. Seek mentors to teach you the ropes on how real life works and how they have been able to move smoothly through it. This means learning more on finances, relationships, work ethic, self-love and faith. Look for books at the library or bookstore. Search videos on talks and apply the things you learn. Just like you have to memorize and learn things at school to pass an exam, you need to learn and apply the things you learned from these resources so you can pass the test of life. So you can live your best life. We are unlimited to our potential. We can never be perfect but we can strive to be, therefore we can never stop learning.

When we love we share the things we know. If you see

your child struggling to tie their shoes, you don't just walk by and go on with your day without stopping and showing them how you tie your shoes. It's the same with anyone. When we learn of ways to make our life easier, better and full of prosperity, we share that. It's selfish to know something as valuable as how to create a budget or how to approach your spouse about a delicate topic and not teach others. Those are the types of things that matter and everyone wants and needs to know. So when you learn how to better your life and how to love, don't forget to spread it out.

When you have owned all these attributes and made them a part of you, you will become this whole new person that is just taking over the world and helping the rest of us heal it. Its truly amazing the changes I have seen in people, including myself. I never thought I would have the courage or motivation to write a book. I am no author and I'm definitely not a very entertaining person. But I have done everything that I have mentioned and the only reason I did it was because I met people I admired, I saw what they did and copied them. I built my dream board and have been doing the things on there little by little. I'm not 60 yet so Dominican Republic is still pending, but I know I will get there. I know that one day I will have a book that millions of people will have read and will talk about how it helped them. Even if this book completely fails, I will just write another, and then another until I get it right. Why? Because time is precious, and no matter what it will keep on going. Whether or not I'm working on my dreams, time will keep on moving without me. So I can either choose to stop dreaming and get a day job I don't really like and be ok with my life or I can push myself to do all these out-of-the-box things and work hard to achieve my dream life using whatever talents I was given. I know I will get to where I need to be, in the meantime I will go where I want go until I get there.

Now its your turn, go for it! Get off your couch and go get your dream board started! No matter what don't stop dreaming. You can fail, you can fall, and when that happens all you have to do is "Dust yourself off and try again." - Aaliyah. The day you stop dreaming, that is the day you will have wasted, because you'll be motivated again anyway. Don't let time pass you by and look back one day and regret not having taken advantage of it.

You working and learning to better yourself and your life is the biggest project you can ever have, the only assignment where the grade matters, it's also the only class that if you fail it will affect not only you but those around you. You can do his, you are the only YOU that exist on this planet, and we all have a calling, purpose or whatever you want to call it, on this earth, in this life. Without you working on you to be who you need to be, the world will never get to where it needs to go.

Now get out there and take over your world!

I Have No Idea What I'm Doing

ABOUT THE AUTHOR

Born and raised in a growing Southern California city called Lancaster to immigrant parents. Candy graduated from California State University, Northridge with a Bachelor of Arts degree in Psychology in 2014.

Having been married at 22, she and her husband, Moroni, have spent their years of marriage learning about themselves and each other and finding ways to grow and become successful in order to help their families and any future members that may come.

After 5 and a half years of marriage Candy and Moroni moved to another state and with no kids and no career path anywhere in sight, she decided to begin her writing career with a blog. After seeing how happy writing made her, she began jotting down ideas for books in all genres.

She is currently working on a children's book with her youngest sister and is really excited to start a strand of self-reliance and motivational books. She is excited to see where her writing takes her and hopes that she can help others find the motivation to follow their dreams, no matter how hard and out of reach they may seem.

I Have No Idea What I'm Doing

Candy Aragon

I Have No Idea What I'm Doing

In case you need this...

"The more you are in a state of gratitude, the more you will attract things to be grateful for"- Walt Disney

"All the adversity I've had in my life, all my troubles and obstacles, have strengthened me... You may not realize it when it happens, but a kick in the teeth may be the best thing in the world for you." - Walt Disney

"A little consideration, a little thought for others, makes all the difference." - Eeyore (*Winnie the Pooh*)

"Just because it's what's done, doesn't mean it's what should be done." - Cinderella (*Cinderella*)

"Sometimes the right path is not the easiest one." -Grandmother Willow (*Pocahontas*)

"The only thing predictable about life is its unpredictability." – Remy (*Ratatouille*)

Life's not a spectator sport. If watchin' is all you're gonna do, then you're gonna watch your life go by without ya." - Laverne (*The Hunchback of Notre Dame*)

"The past can hurt. But the way I see it, you can either run from it or learn from it." - Rafiki (*The Lion King*)

"Happiness is the richest thing we will ever own" –Donald Duck

Because Disney is life....... =)

Candy Aragon

Made in the USA
San Bernardino, CA
16 January 2019